The mango tree

Written by Jamila Gavin

Illustrated by Rhian Nest James

Heinemann

Grandma was on the garden bench.
She looked up at the sky.
'The sun is like a yellow mango,'
she said to Amina.

‘Did you have mangoes in Pakistan?’
said Amina.
‘Yes,’ said Grandma.
‘I wish we had a mango tree here.’

Amina went to see Grandpa.
'Have we got a mango tree?' she said.
'No, we have not got a mango tree,'
said Grandpa.
'But we have got a cherry tree.'

'I have a mango stone,' said Ali.
'I will put it in the ground.
Then we will have a mango tree and
Grandma will have mangoes to eat.'

So Ali put the mango stone
in the ground.
'I will make a wish,' said Ali.
'I wish for a mango tree.'

Ali and Amina looked for the mango tree but it did not come up. ‘I wish Grandma could have a mango tree,’ said Ali.

Grandpa, Ali and Amina went
to the supermarket.
They looked for some mangoes.
There were apples, pears and bananas
but there were no mangoes.

Then they went to the market.
'I can see some mangoes,' said Amina.
'So can I,' said Ali.
Grandpa got a bag of mangoes.

Grandpa, Ali and Amina went home.
'Put the mangoes on the cherry tree,'
said Grandpa.
Ali and Amina made the cherry tree
into a mango tree.

‘Grandma,’ called Ali.
‘Grandma,’ called Amina.
‘There is a mango tree
in the garden.’

Grandma looked at the tree.
'Now I have a mango tree,
just like I had in Pakistan,'
she said.